AF327191

# The Nonessential Thread
## Brocade, Silks to Synthetics

Lotus Stack

The Minneapolis Institute of Arts

This book was produced in conjunction with the exhibition
"The Nonessential Thread: Brocade, Silks to Synthetics,"
held at The Minneapolis Institute of Arts, 2 September to
29 October 1989.

Designed by Anne Knauff
Edited by Elisabeth Sövik and Leslie Reindl
Photographs by Gary Mortensen
Line drawings by Abby Sue Fisher



Library of Congress Catalog Card Number 89-62658
International Standard Book Number 0-912964-39-1

This publication was funded in part by the Andrew W.
Mellon Foundation and by a grant from the National
Endowment for the Arts, a federal agency.

Cover illustration:
*Denkheb* (bedcovering)
Bhutan, 20th century
Wool
Gift of N. Bud Grossman   82.102.29

# Contents

# Preface

This is the third in a series of books on the textile collection of The Minneapolis Institute of Arts. Each one presents a technique of cloth-making and discusses its use by various cultures throughout history. Besides introducing the museum's textile holdings, these publications provide general information that will help readers appreciate other textiles they may encounter.

*The Nonessential Thread* explains how supplementary threads are incorporated into a woven structure to create brocaded cloth. It is not a complete survey of all brocaded textiles but covers brocade production only in those geographical areas where pieces in the museum's collection originated. Thus, for example, it does not deal with the famous pre-Columbian brocades from South America. For readers interested in pursuing the topic further, a brief bibliography is included. A summary of the museum's brocade holdings appears in the Appendix.

My initial consideration of technical and historical concepts was broadened and refined through discussions with a number of artists, weavers, and textile historians. I am especially grateful to Nobuko Kajatani, Suzanne Baizerman, Morgan Clifford, Laura Foster Nicholson, John Vollmer, and Elizabeth Barber.

For their efforts in the preparation of this catalogue and exhibition I extend special thanks to Mary Ann Butterfield, Peggy Dorwick, Beverly Hussian, Janet Johnson, Virginia Hjelmstad, Elizabeth Olson, and Maureen Hark of the textiles department; Elisabeth Sövik and Leslie Reindl, editors; Roxy Ballard and Anne Knauff, designers; Gwen Bitz, registrar, and Karen Duncan, associate registrar; Gary Mortensen and Robert Fogt, photographers; Patrick Atherton, typesetter; Steven Williams, lighting technician; and Tom Jance, Patti Landres, William Skodgi, Charles Foster, and Brian Stieler, exhibition technicians. Evan Maurer, director; Timothy Fiske, associate director; and Michael Conforti, chief curator, have supported this project with enthusiasm. Funding for the exhibition and catalogue was organized by Beth Desnick. Lisa Nebenzahl and James Ockuly, of the museum's media department, produced the video complement to the exhibition. I especially appreciate Edward Stack's continuing support throughout the catalogue writing and exhibition development. Finally, I wish to express my gratitude to Tom and Donna Slocum, John and Susan Michelman, Edward Stack, Mary Ann Butterfield, and Morgan Clifford, whose generous loans have enhanced this exhibition immeasurably.

# Introduction

Today, cloth is usually taken for granted, but this attitude is fairly new. Until the nineteenth century, all fabric was made by hand from fibers gathered laboriously from the land or obtained from animals. Next to agriculture, textile production was the most labor-intensive activity of humankind.

Cloth production undoubtedly originated to meet basic physical needs. However, it satisfied aesthetic needs as well. As weaving technology developed, weavers devised many different textile structures appropriate for the diverse purposes their cloth was to serve.

One woven structure used for patterned cloth in many parts of the world is brocade. The term *brocade*, as used in textile literature, has various interpretations. Here it is used to mean any patterned cloth that has been woven with supplementary, or structurally nonessential, threads. That is, removal of the pattern threads would not alter the essential structure of the cloth. In this respect brocaded textiles are similar to embroidered cloth. A primary difference between them is that the brocade weaver incorporates the pattern threads as the fabric is being woven on the loom, whereas the embroiderer adds the pattern threads (usually with a needle or some other piercing tool) to fabric already woven.

Brocading is one of the simplest ways to weave a multicolored patterned fabric. The loom can be very basic; however, even with complex woven structures made on complicated looms, brocading may be used to introduce additional color in the form of discontinuous supplementary wefts. Metallic threads have often been incorporated in this manner because the resulting fabric is lighter weight and less costly than if metal were used throughout.

Because textiles are so perishable, few pieces of ancient cloth have survived, and so we do not know when the brocade structure was first developed. Although patterning with supplementary threads was certainly not done on the first fabrics to be made, the few brocaded burial cloths found at sites in Peru, Europe, and the Middle East indicate that the brocade structure has been in use for about five thousand years.

Textile fragments with weft float brocading have been found in Switzerland in late Neolithic dwellings dating from about 3000 to 2500 B.C. Since archaeological evidence suggests that weaving in that culture was influenced by the same textile tradition on which Greek weaving was based, it is quite possible that at least some ancient Greek patterned cloth was brocaded.

Linen cloth of very fine quality found in tombs of the early Middle Kingdom (1900 B.C.) indicates that Egyptian weavers knew how to do inlay brocade. The selvages of many of these textiles have decorative fringes made by inlay brocading, and this technique was occasionally used for "weavers' marks" identifying the origin of the cloth.

In Peru, where a complex weaving tradition developed well before the beginning of the Christian era, brocade was not initially a popular cloth structure. However, there is evidence that it was produced there at least as early as 500 B.C.

The brocade structure was not employed in the Far East until relatively late. China had a very old tradition of making patterned textiles with complex woven structures; it was not until the T'ang dynasty (A.D. 618–906), when China was strongly influenced by the Middle East and central Asia, that the simpler structure of brocade was adopted by Chinese weavers.

Brocaded textiles have always had many uses. Depending on the type of fiber and the thickness of the threads, brocades can range from heavy, durable rugs to delicate dress fabrics. The brocaded textiles in the collection of The Minneapolis Institute of Arts display the variety of this particular type of patterned cloth.

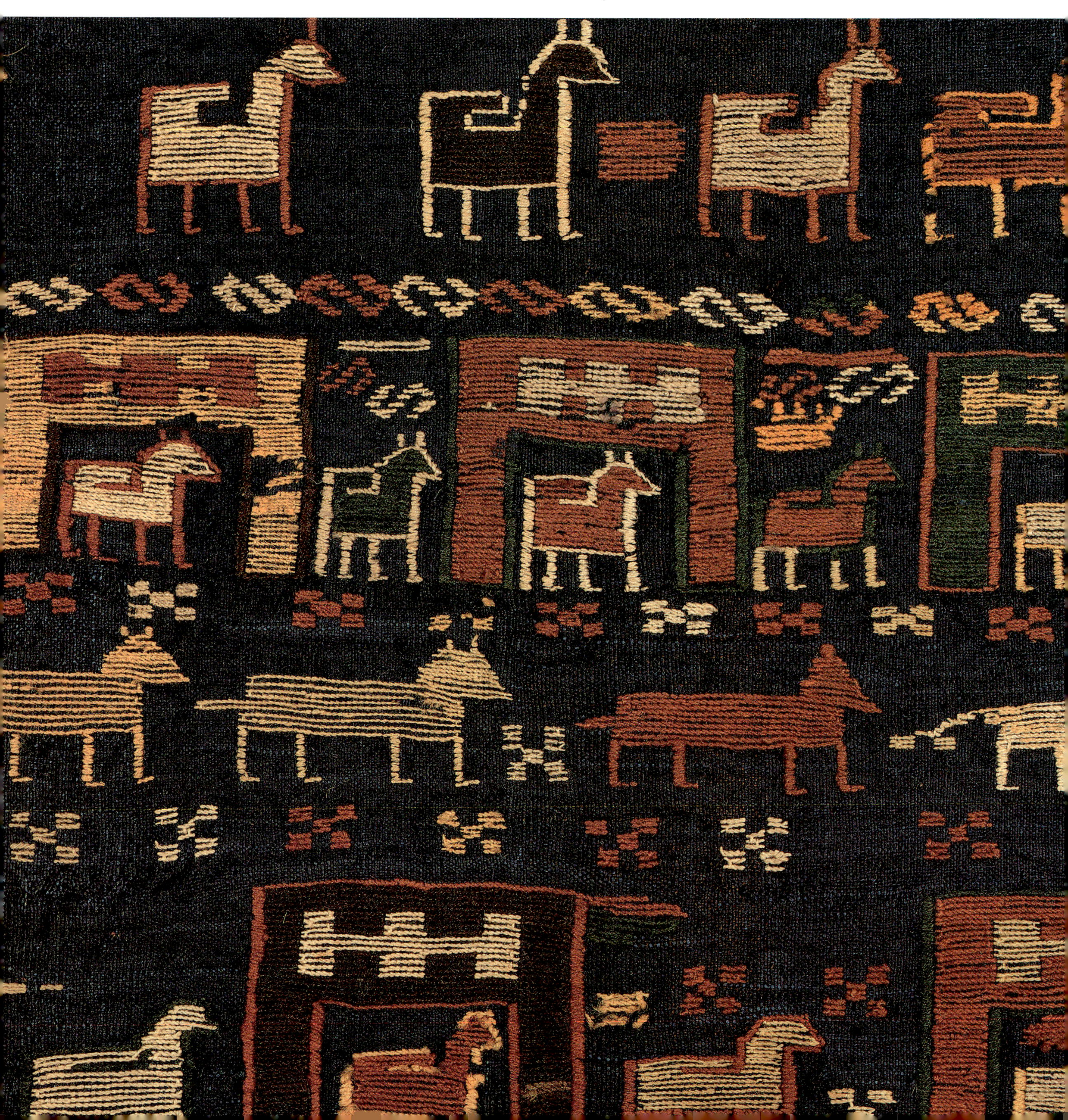

# The Middle East

The Middle East is home to two distinct weaving traditions: the urban and the nomadic. In general, weavers in the cities are men, working in small workshops. Nomadic weavers are almost always women. The professional weaver in the city usually specializes in a particular type of cloth and produces fabric that will be used by the purchaser. The nomadic weaver, often as skilled in her art as the city professional, weaves primarily to fulfill her family's household needs. As time and circumstances permit, she creates a surplus that can be sold in nearby markets. Each tradition has a long history, and each has adapted to political, economic, and social changes.

Until the twentieth century, nomadic migrations were an important part of life in much of the Middle East. The textiles most commonly associated with this tradition are pile rugs and *kilims.* However, brocaded fabrics were also used, for such items as lightweight floor coverings, cushion covers, carrying sacks, room dividers, and animal trappings. For the most part, these were made of wool from sheep and goats that was gathered and spun when the animals were being pastured.

The most widely used brocade structures are the weft float (*cicim* and *zili*) and weft wrapping (*soumak*). Individual tribes have often modified each structure slightly and established their own distinctive techniques. The most durable brocaded cloth is that made by means of weft wrapping, but it is also the most time-consuming to produce. Sometimes the patterning is so thick that it completely covers the ground cloth; on other fabrics, design motifs are scattered sparsely over the entire field.

There are few old examples of these types of textiles because they were made to be used and, though they were valued, were considered utilitarian fabrics, not luxury goods. Weavers created patterns to enliven the interiors of tents and add beauty to life in general. Decorative animal trappings, like the one pictured here from the Caucasus area of southwestern Russia, were used on special occasions, such as weddings.

The most famous textiles from urban workshops are silks with a complex structure and silk damask fabrics. Many textile historians believe that the Middle East was the area where the basic drawloom, as we know it today, originated. This type of loom was probably developed in the seventh century. It was the fabrics created on these looms, which soon were in use throughout the Islamic world, that inspired the development of the European silk industry, which began in Italy in the late Middle Ages.

Opposite: *Kira* (woman's wraparound dress)
Bhutan, about 1970
Cotton, silk and metallic threads
Gift of N. Bud Grossman   81.50

Below: detail

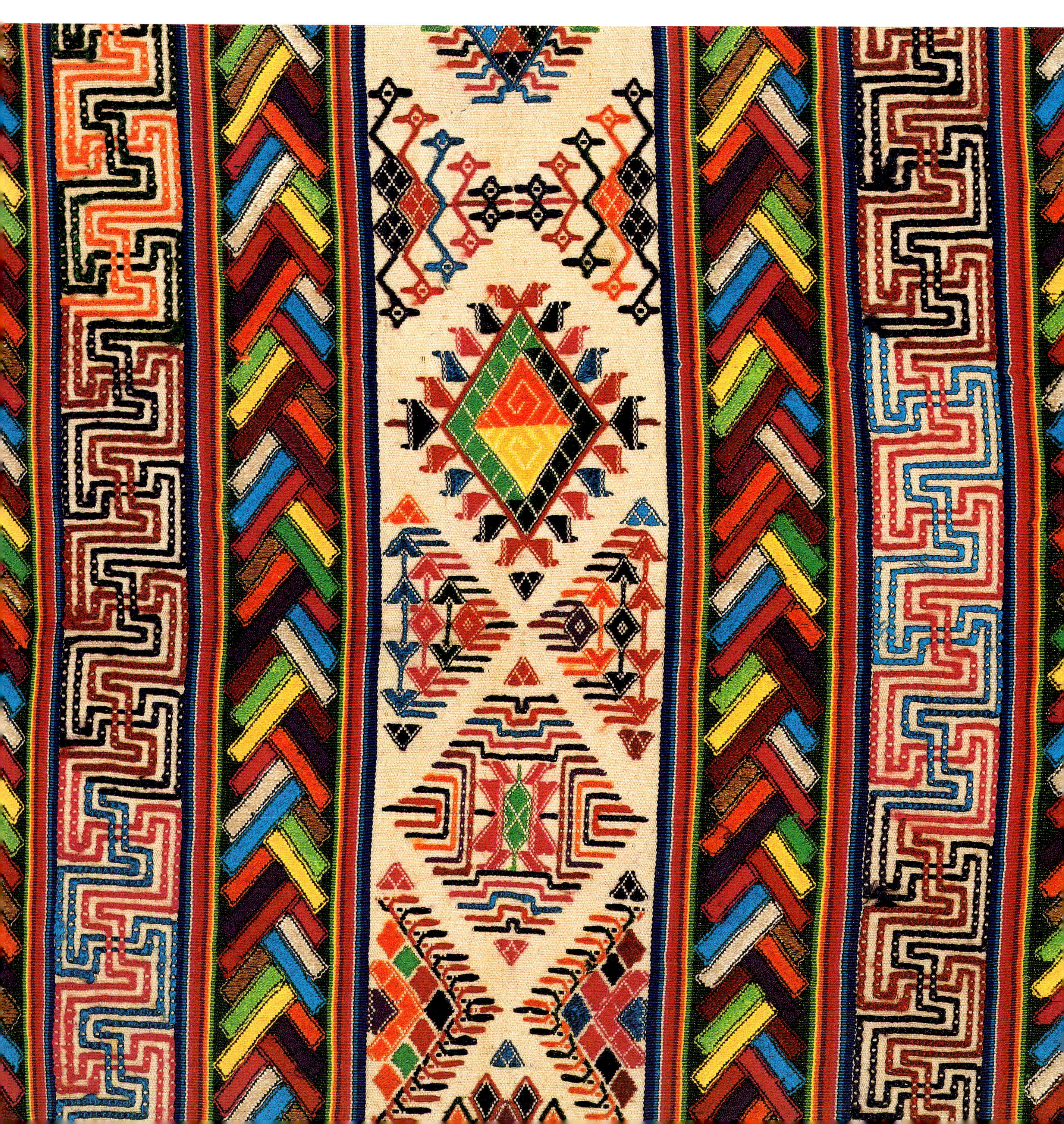

# South Asia

Throughout the south Asian subcontinent, the brocade structure is widely used in weaving patterned cloth. Historically, the best-known centers of brocaded production are Banaras, in India, and Dacca, formerly in India and now in Bangladesh.

## India

Banaras (sometimes referred to by its older name, Varanasi) is thought by some scholars to be the oldest city continuously occupied to the present day. The brocaded silk saris made there, particularly those with metallic threads, are famous not only in India itself but also far beyond that country's border.

The production of these silk fabrics is highly sophisticated, requiring the cooperation of many skilled craftsmen. In addition to the spinning and coloring of the fine silk threads, there is a process for making metallic threads.

Some of India's expert metalworkers specialize in silver and gold threads. Beginning with fine metal wire that has been made for the purpose, the craftsman pounds the wire into thin, flat, flexible strips, which then are wound around a core thread, usually silk. The color chosen for the core thread depends on the alloy used for the strips or on the finish applied to them. Sometimes strips are coated with a wash of a different metal, so that, for example, a metal strip of a silver alloy may appear to be gold. Yellow and red cores are used to create various shades of gold threads; white is the usual core color for silver threads. The color of the core is important because the metal strip is wound in a spiral through which portions of the thread are visible. How much core shows depends on how densely the metal strip is wound. The more core thread exposed, the less metal strip required and the more economical the thread—though the effect is somewhat less spectacular.

The most intricate brocading requires a pattern control device, or *naksha*, which is attached to the loom

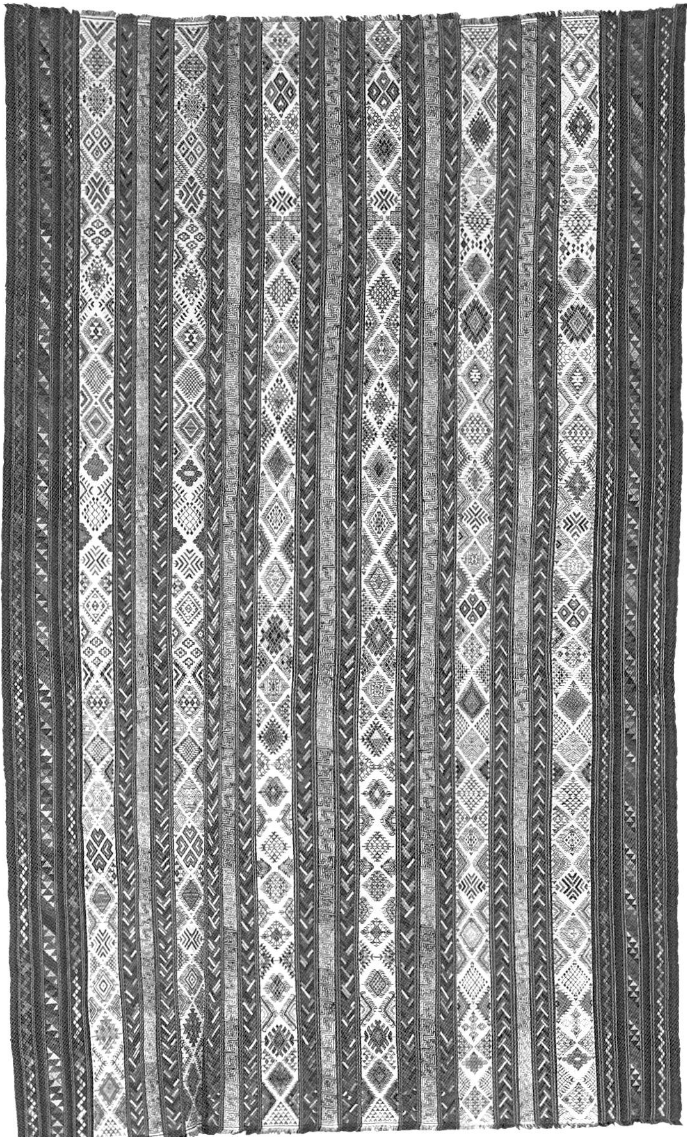

before weaving begins. The *nakshas* of Banaras have made that city famous as a weaving center. The tradition among the Banaras weavers is that the first *naksha bandhas*, or brocade pattern tyers, were Islamic Persians who came to India at the end of the thirteenth century. At one time these specialists were to be found in many of the Mogul imperial weaving workshops located throughout the northern part of the country, but today the most skilled are in Banaras. They will sometimes make the *nakshas* for other brocade centers, such as those in Surat and Chanderi. A *naksha* can be stored and re-attached to the loom when that particular pattern is wanted.

In spite of competition from industrial production, the handweaving brocade tradition continues to this day in Banaras. Although there are not as many weavers as in the past, luxury silks of high quality still are made.

## Bangladesh

Historically, the best-known Indian textiles were cotton fabrics. India's weaving tradition was built on cotton, and the most famous center of production was Dacca, in eastern Bengal, today the country of Bangladesh. Dacca fabrics attained their greatest refinement during the Mogul period, when they became so expensive that only the very wealthy could afford them. This muslin was so lightweight and fine that the literature of the time described it with such poetic names as *abrawan* (running water), *bafthawa* (woven air), and *shabnam* (evening dew). During the seventeenth century a fifteen-square-yard piece could weigh as little as two ounces. The most highly regarded of the Dacca cottons was the *jamdani*, or brocaded muslin, made with discontinuous supplementary wefts.

Like the brocaded silk of Banaras, the brocaded Dacca muslins required a great deal of specialized labor. Moreover, the fine cotton thread could be manipulated only in the early morning and late afternoon, when the humidity was high. If the air was too dry, the fragile threads would break. Both the spinners and the weavers needed great skill, for the special qualities of the cloth were due equally to the fineness of the thread and the expertise of the weaver. During the nineteenth century, when quality was considered to be declining, spinners were still getting 250 miles of thread to the pound!

Unlike the patterning in the Banaras brocades, the patterning in the Dacca brocades was not loom controlled, so there was no need for a *naksha bandha*. The *jamdani* weaver usually followed a paper pattern of the design. The patterns were often intricate and the colors usually rather subdued. To speed up production, two weavers frequently worked side by side on the same loom.

Today brocaded cotton fabrics are still woven in Dacca, but the very finest muslins are no longer made. It is not economically feasible to spin and weave by hand, and machines cannot produce cloth of the same quality.

## Bhutan

Bhutan, the small Himalayan country to the east and north of India, has a rich weaving tradition that is an integral part of the culture. Until about twenty years ago, this tradition was almost unknown to the Western world. The highly skilled Bhutanese weavers produced primarily for themselves and to supply the needs of a domestic market.

As in many other societies that are not predominantly urban, in Bhutan social status, wealth, regional identification, and self-esteem are closely tied to textile production and use. Most of the weaving is done by women for their own family's needs, although some work is commissioned. Women learn their skills at an early age from their mothers or other female relatives.

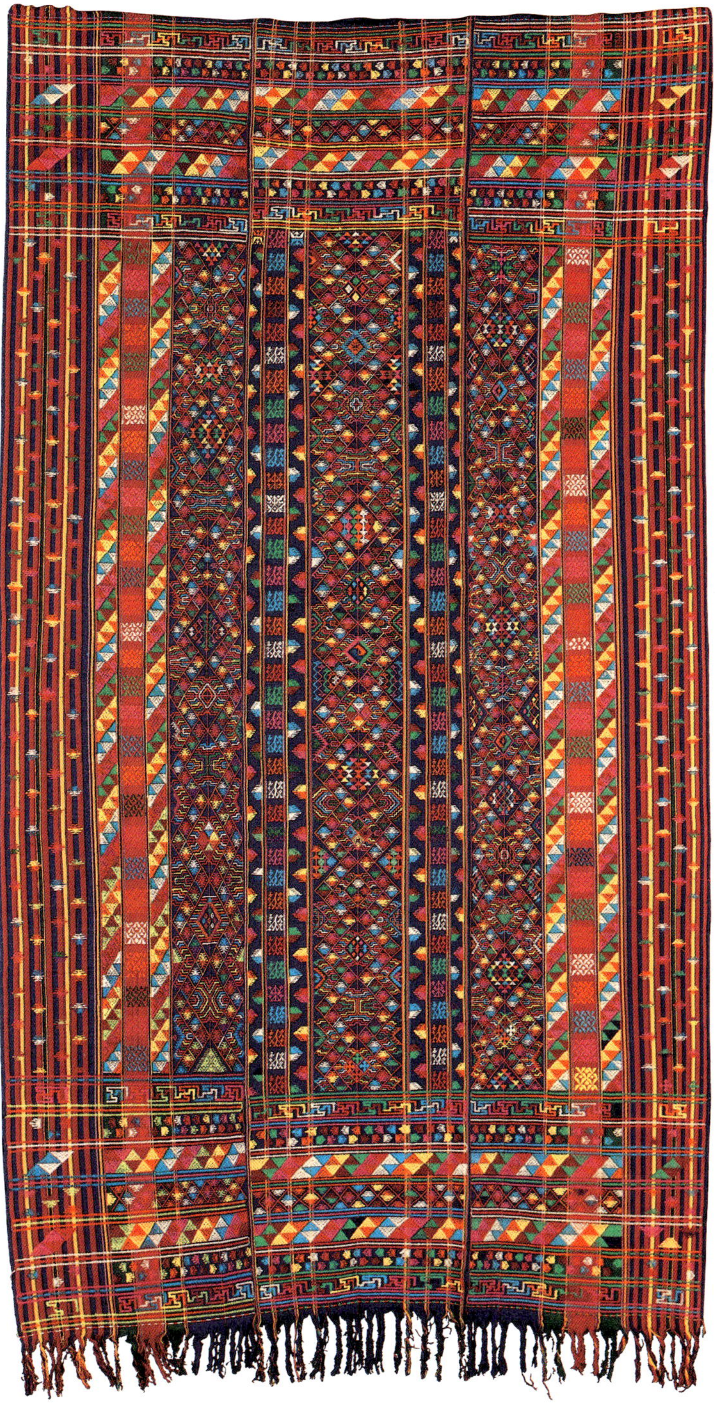

There seem to be two weaving traditions, both of which include elaborate brocaded fabrics.

Wool weaving is generally done on a small horizontal loom used to produce a twill ground cloth. These wool fabrics resemble certain types of Tibetan cloth and their production undoubtedly has been influenced by the proximity of Bhutan to Tibet. Today much of the woolen cloth is woven in central Bhutan, where some weavers also make brocaded belts by means of a tablet-weaving technique in which the cards that form the shedding mechanism are made from X-ray film.

In eastern Bhutan, an area renowned for fine weaving, a body-tension loom is used to create both cotton and silk textiles for men's and women's clothing and for other domestic and ceremonial purposes. Warp and weft float and inlay brocade are used extensively. Other, less common methods are also employed to incorporate supplementary weft pattern threads, and these give Bhutanese textiles a highly distinctive character. Some of the most elaborate brocades are woven as *kira*, women's dresses. Worn as a wraparound garment, the *kira* is a large rectangle made up of three panels of brocaded warp-faced ground cloth. In general, the best of these untailored garments are made entirely of cotton, or of raw silk and cotton, and brocaded with discontinuous supplementary threads of silk. One of the few tailored garments used by the Bhutanese is the *kho*, a man's coat. The more elaborate ones are made of silk and patterned with a warp float brocade.

Weaving is seen as an essential part of Bhutanese culture, and the government encourages the wearing of traditional costume. This policy almost guarantees the continuance of handweaving. Although commercially spun and synthetic yarns are now widely used, handweaving is thriving in Bhutan today.

# The Far East

## China

Chinese weavers began creating elaborately patterned silk fabrics during the early Han dynasty (206 B.C.–A.D. 220). Many of these textiles—which were used for clothing, for ceremonial and domestic purposes, and also for trade—were made by professional weavers in government and private workshops located in various cities throughout the country.

The brocade structure (supplementary weft patterning) was introduced during the late T'ang dynasty (618–906), when brocaded fabrics woven on Western draw-looms were brought to China via Persian or central Asian trade routes. Previously, most of the patterned cloth produced by Chinese weavers had a complex warp structure. Although very beautiful, these fabrics were severely limited as to variations of pattern and color once the loom setup had been established. With supplementary weft patterning, however, the weaver could easily add a variety of colors to a single woven panel.

Representations of looms and costumes on jars found in tombs suggest that Chinese peasant weavers also used the brocade structure for simple patterning at quite an early date. To this day, peasant weavers belonging to minority groups living in southwestern China make brocaded fabrics of cotton and silk on a body-tension pattern-rod loom.

From the eleventh through the mid-seventeenth century, supplementary weft patterning was the favored structure for the finest and most elaborate Chinese silk textiles. Costly threads and intricate patterns provided a means of displaying the taste, position, and wealth of those who could afford to own such fabrics. At court and in private life, brocaded textiles were used for costume and for domestic needs. In religious festivals and celebrations, they served as altar frontals, banners, and priests' robes.

During the Ming period (1368–1643), workshop production was intensive, and the government established imperial production centers in several cities of the empire. For the most part these workshops supplied the court, but occasionally weavers were allowed to sell their cloth privately. Private workshops, which were usually much smaller than the government establishments, also wove brocades. During the later Ming period, trade with Europe was opened up, initially by Portuguese shippers, and large quantities of silk textiles, mainly of lesser quality, were produced for this market. This trade has continued to the present and has had a considerable effect on the Chinese economy. Fashion changes in dress and in household decor in the West have sometimes resulted in labor shortages or surpluses in China, leading to periods of inflation or economic depression.

During the Ch'ing period (1644–1912), workshop specialization in silk manufacturing continued to increase. Brocaded textiles were still produced for the court and private sector, but now tapestry and embroidery were preferred for the very finest of fabrics.

## Japan

As with a number of other textile techniques, the Japanese apparently learned supplementary weft patterning from the Chinese and Koreans. However, they developed it into a striking textile art form that is distinctively Japanese.

The brocades of the Momoyama period (1573–1615) were particularly lavish. This period was a time of economic expansion for Japan. A growing merchant class was eager to display

Woman's coat
China, 17th century
Silk
The John R. Van Derlip Fund   42.8.5

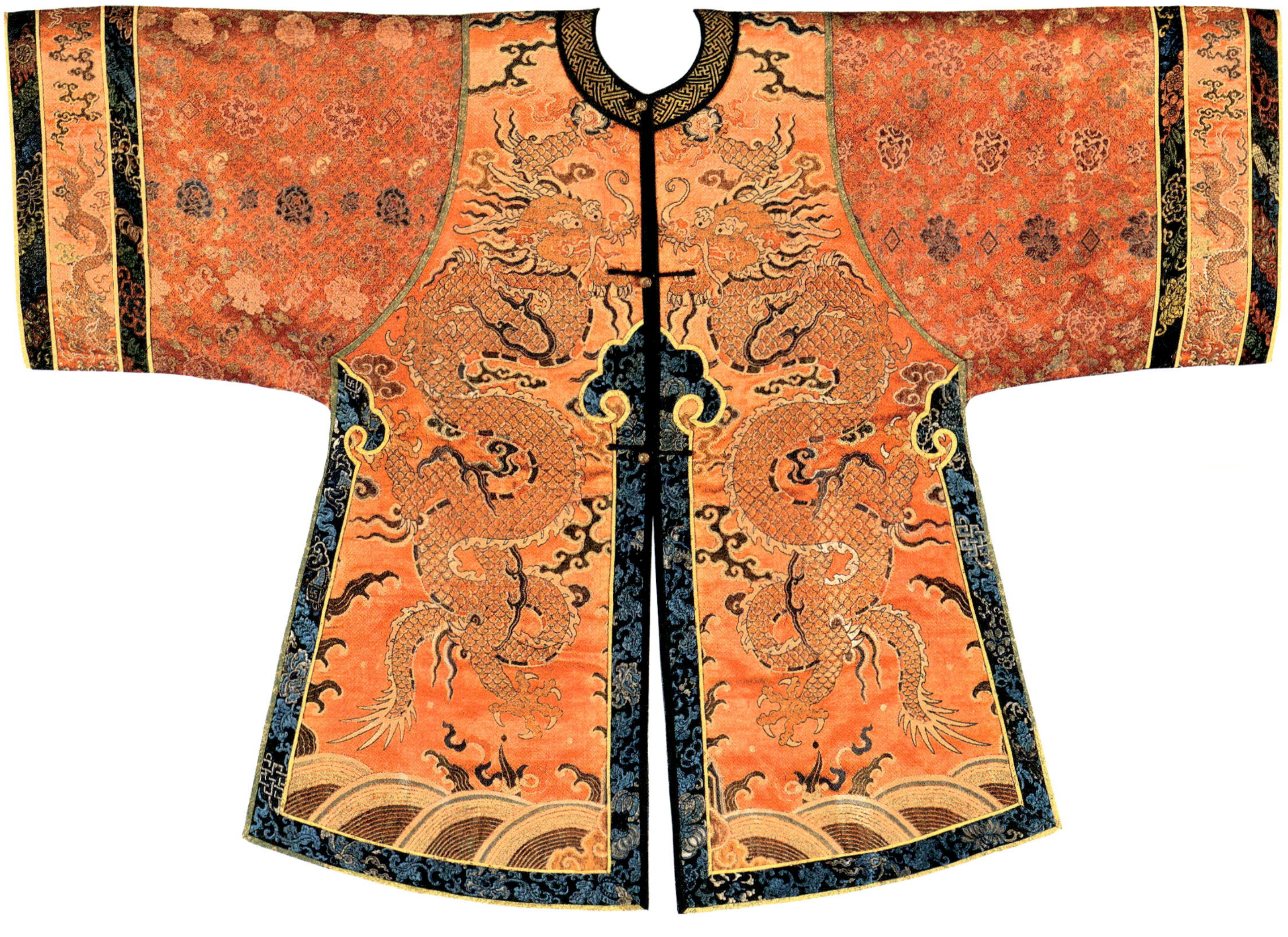

*Tampan* (ceremonial cloth), detail
Indonesia, 19th century
Cotton
Gift of Roberta and Richard Simmons   88.103.2

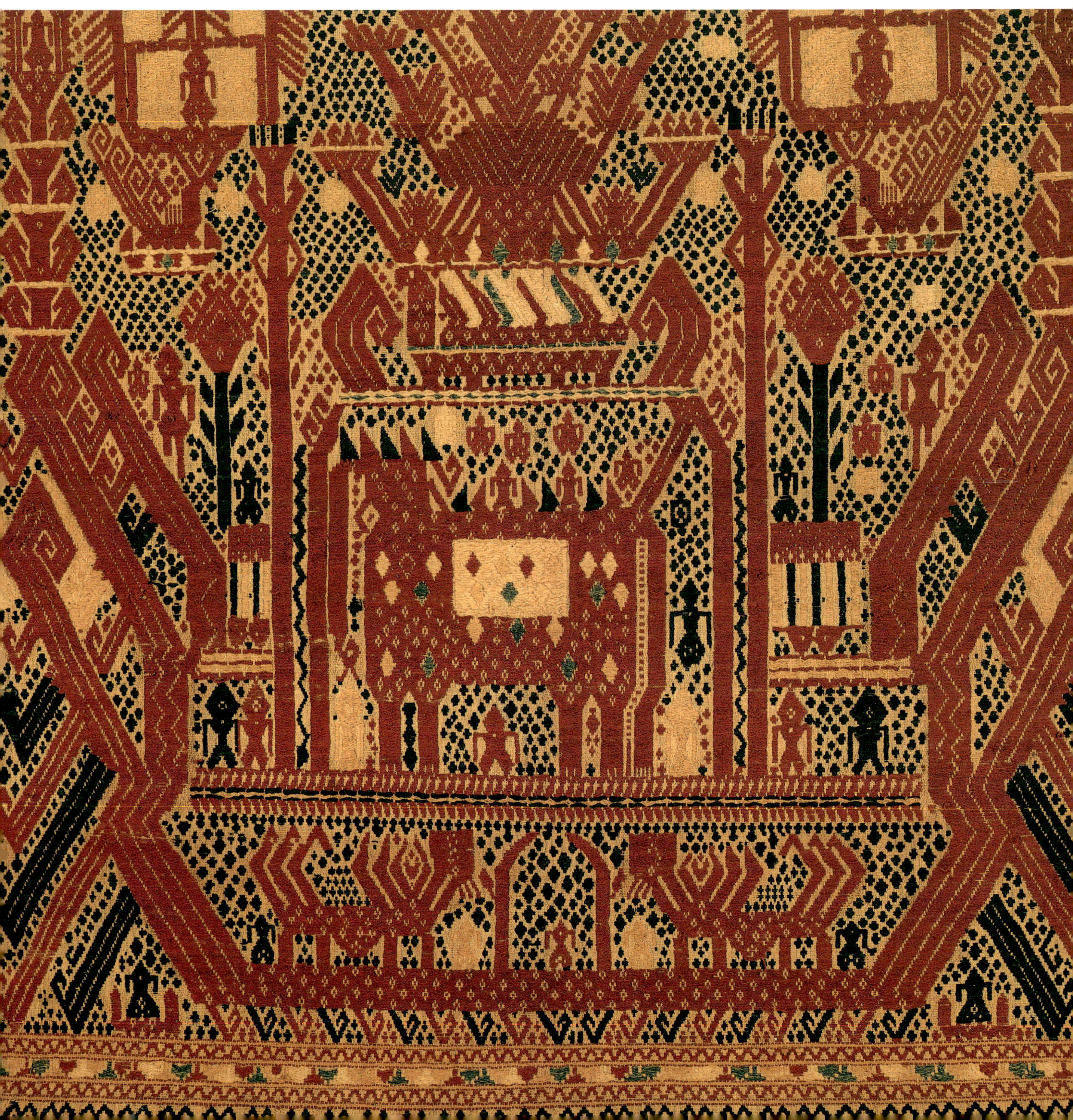

newly acquired wealth and status, and textile producers seized the opportunity to create elaborate and costly costume fabrics. As the primary woven structure for polychrome fabrics, supplementary weft patterning became very popular. The famous *kara-ori* costume used in No theater performances developed out of brocade imitations of richly embroidered Chinese Ming textiles. The costliness of Momoyama brocades was due to labor-intensive manufacture and, even more, to the use of gold, silver, and other expensive threads.

Throughout the Edo period (1615–1867), brocades continued to be made, but their production was affected by governmental shifts from extreme extravagance to stern repression of all luxury. At times, sumptuary laws prohibited townspeople from wearing brocades. The weavers of patterned cloth suffered in consequence, although those who specialized in dyeing and printing benefited from laws aimed at controlling the use of costly threads in textile manufacturing.

Today some brocaded textiles are still produced in Japan, mainly for the *obi* belt worn with the traditional woman's dress, the *kimono*.

## Indonesia

The best-known Indonesian brocades are the cotton cloths and richly patterned silk fabrics woven on the island of Sumatra. Perhaps most familiar in the West are the "ship cloths," which are made primarily in the Lampong region of southern Sumatra. These are of three types, the most common being the *tampan*—a square cotton cloth brocaded with a reddish brown or reddish brown and blue supplementary weft. Some of the patterns resemble ships, but most are geometric. Like many Indonesian textiles, the *tampan* is often used in ceremonial celebrations. At marriages, the bride frequently sits on a *tampan* and uses others as gift wrappers.

Silk weaving is thought to have developed in Sumatra sometime after A.D. 1000, as a result of the India–China trade. Gold-brocaded red silk fabrics are made in the Palembang region on the eastern coast and have always been considered a luxury cloth. They are used primarily as clothing. Unlike the *tampan*, which is no longer woven, these silk brocades are still being produced in small workshops.

Supplementary weft patterning is used in a number of other areas of Indonesia in addition to Sumatra. It is often combined with other techniques, such as embroidery and *ikat* (a resist dye technique), to create strikingly elaborate patterned textiles.

Opposite: *Blanket*
Niamey, Niger, 20th century
Cotton and synthetic
Gift of Roberta and Richard Simmons   86.100.4

Below: detail

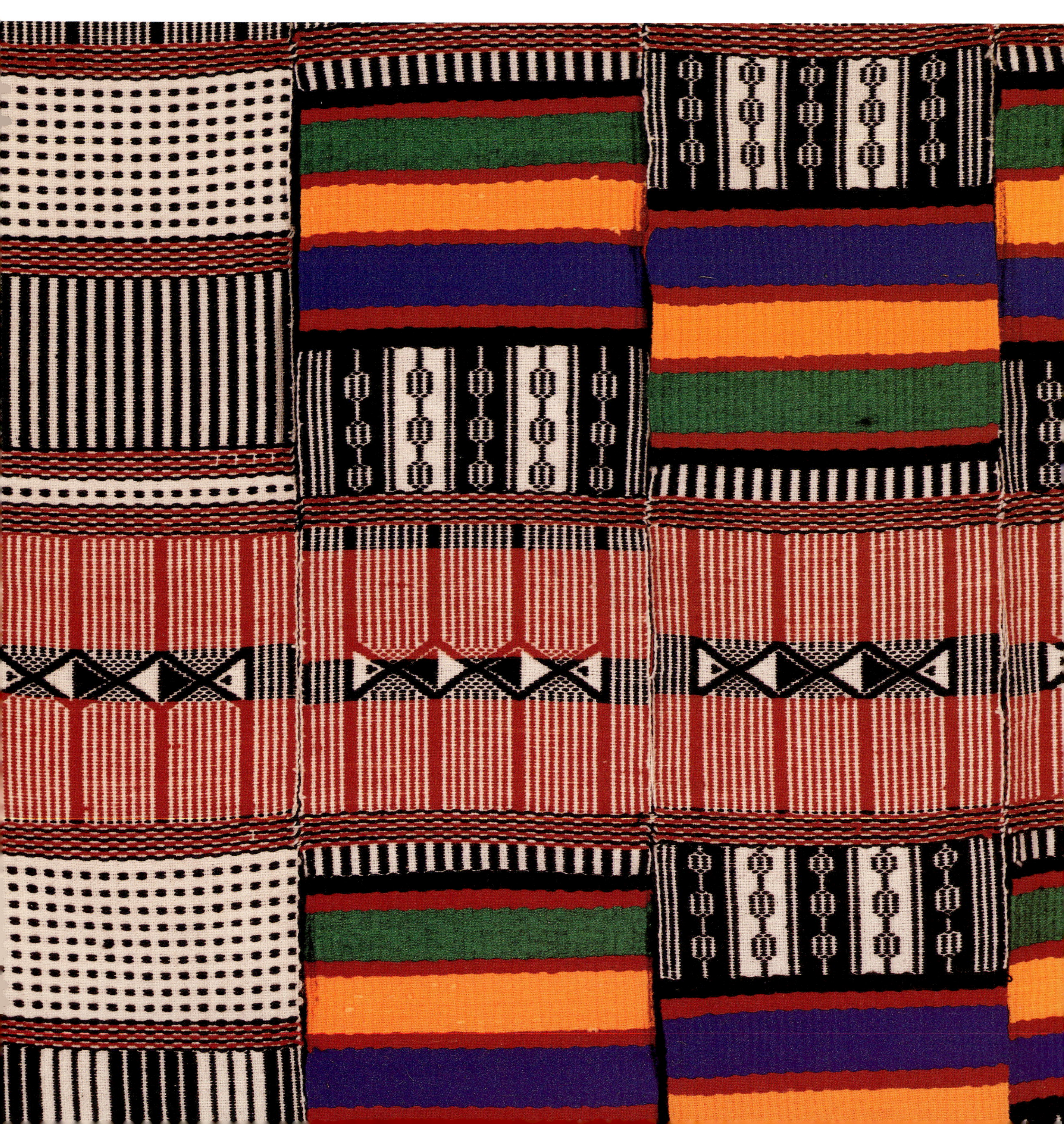

# West Africa

West Africa, the region south of the Sahara from the Ivory Coast to Lake Chad, has a rich textile tradition that is important economically and socially to the various peoples living there. The cloth sections in the town markets are always large, with imported and domestic machine-woven fabrics for sale, as well as handwoven textiles. Among the handwoven items are many types of brocades; in West Africa the most common way to weave patterned fabrics is with the use of supplementary wefts. Inlay brocade is favored both by men who work professionally in weaving sheds, making cloth for the market or royal commissions, and by women weaving at home for their families.

West Africa's most famous brocades are the striking strip-woven cloths, which are made by men using a distinctive type of horizontal loom. The best known are the *kente* cloths woven by the Ashanti people of Ghana, but these fine silk brocades are only one of many types of narrow strip-woven fabrics with supplementary weft patterning that are produced throughout West Africa.

Strip-woven cloth consists of a series of long, narrow strips, one to twelve inches wide, sewn together along their selvages. The number of strips depends on the purpose of the finished fabric. Strip-woven fabric is used for clothing (shawls, head cloths, belts, shirts, pants) and also for domestic textiles (blankets, rugs, pillows, tent dividers). It is made in various grades, from sparsely patterned wool and cotton cloths to the highly decorated silk wrappers worn by the nobility.

Cloth from burial sites in Mali indicates that the tradition of strip-woven textiles goes back at least to the eleventh century. Cotton and wool, fibers native to the region, have been employed in these fabrics for centuries. Imported silk is a later addition. Silk threads for weaving were initially obtained from imported silk cloth. Like the weavers of ancient Rome who unraveled Chinese silk cloth to obtain the precious threads, West African weavers reused the silk yarns as supplementary wefts. Cotton, wool, and silk remain in use in West Africa today, along with rayon and other synthetics.

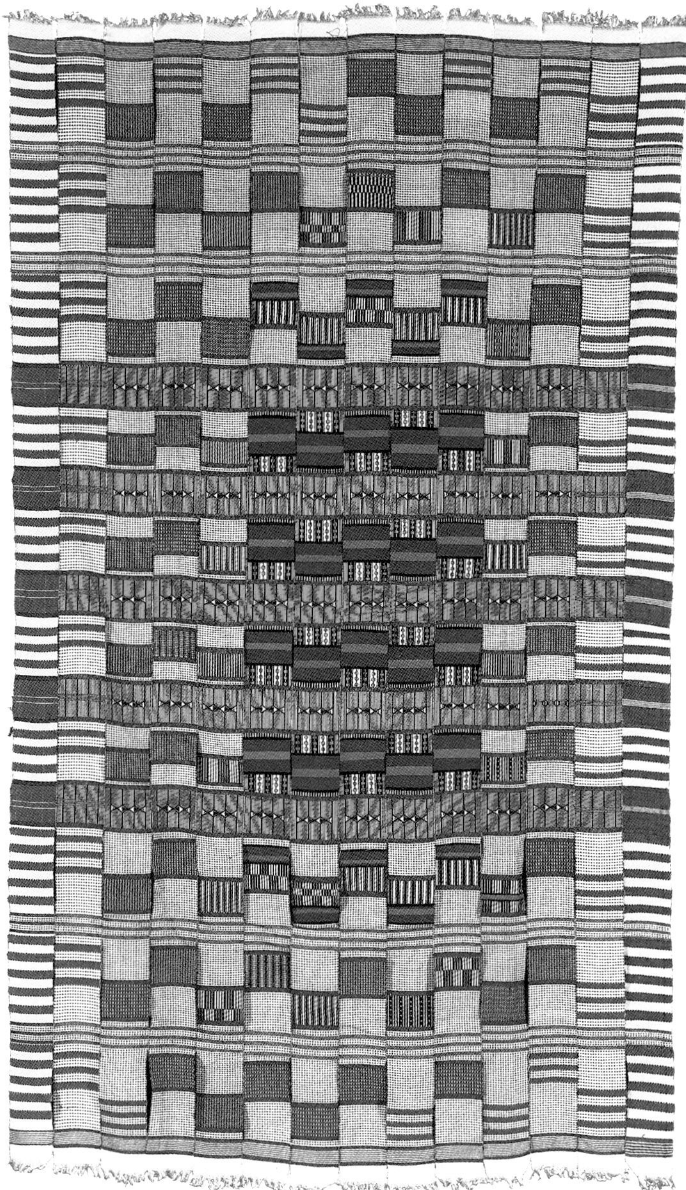

# Europe

## Italy

Some of the oldest brocades in the collection of The Minneapolis Institute of Arts were woven in Italy in the sixteenth and seventeenth centuries. They are simple white linen towels with a blue cotton supplementary weft float pattern.

The production of blue-and-white brocaded linens (tablecloths, napkins, towels, altar cloths) in the Umbrian region of Italy has a long tradition. Representations of these cloths in Italian frescoes and European paintings and tapestries of the fifteenth and sixteenth centuries attest to their popularity with the upper classes. Sometime during the seventeenth century, these textiles ceased to be symbols of wealth, but production continued (although in a less refined form) to the beginning of the twentieth century.

The prototypes for these brocaded cloths are thought to have been elaborately embroidered towels made in convent workshops in Tuscany during the thirteenth century. Not for the first or the last time in the annals of textile history, weavers adapted the look of another textile form, in this case embroidery, to produce a "new" patterned cloth. By the fourteenth century Umbria, particularly the area around Perugia, had become the center of this style, and to this day the towels are known as Perugian towels. Many of these cloths were made by men and women working at looms in their homes, whose weaving was carried on in addition to agricultural and domestic duties. The finest examples, however, most likely were woven by full-time guild weavers, usually men, who worked in small workshops in the city.

Linen fiber, used for the threads of the ground cloth, was grown extensively in Europe. Cotton, used for the pattern threads, was imported by sea and overland routes. The finest cotton came from Hama in Syria and Alexandria in Egypt, and a cheaper variety came from Turkey. In Perugia the cotton was spun into a soft brocading thread and then dyed blue, at first with woad and later with imported indigo. After the brocaded fabric was woven it was sent to the finishers, highly trained professional craftsmen who carried out such procedures as washing, sizing, and flattening the cloth. By the end of the fourteenth century, extensive trade routes linked Perugia with many parts of Europe, and the finished towels were sent north to France, Flanders, and Germany, as well as to other cities in Italy.

During the late Middle Ages, Italy became a major producer of wool and cotton cloth, which was sold throughout the Mediterranean world. Contact with Islamic culture, especially in Spain and Sicily and the Crusader states, gave the Italians a greater knowledge of silk-weaving techniques and production methods. In the early Renaissance period, Italy became a major producer of silk cloth, and many of the Italian city-states became important suppliers of luxury textiles to the rest of Europe.

## France

Beyond their intrinsic aesthetic value, beautiful textiles, because of their costliness, symbolized wealth and the power associated with wealth. As the royal courts of Europe became more sophisticated, so too did the sense of fashion. "Costly thy habit as thy purse can buy" (as Shakespeare phrased it) was the rule. Courtiers wanted to dress so as to show their importance. Outfitting himself and his wife for a single important court appearance could amount to as much as 25 percent of a young nobleman's household expenses (which also included the maintenance of several servants and a modest stable). Clothing expenditures were thus significant in a country's economy, particularly if much of the clothing was made from imported fabrics.

*Towel*, detail
Perugia, Italy, 16th century
Cotton and linen
Gift of Mrs. C. C. Bovey   22.1.6

*Dress fabric*, detail
France, 18th century
Silk
Anonymous gift, by exchange, and the
Miscellaneous Purchase Fund   84.16.12

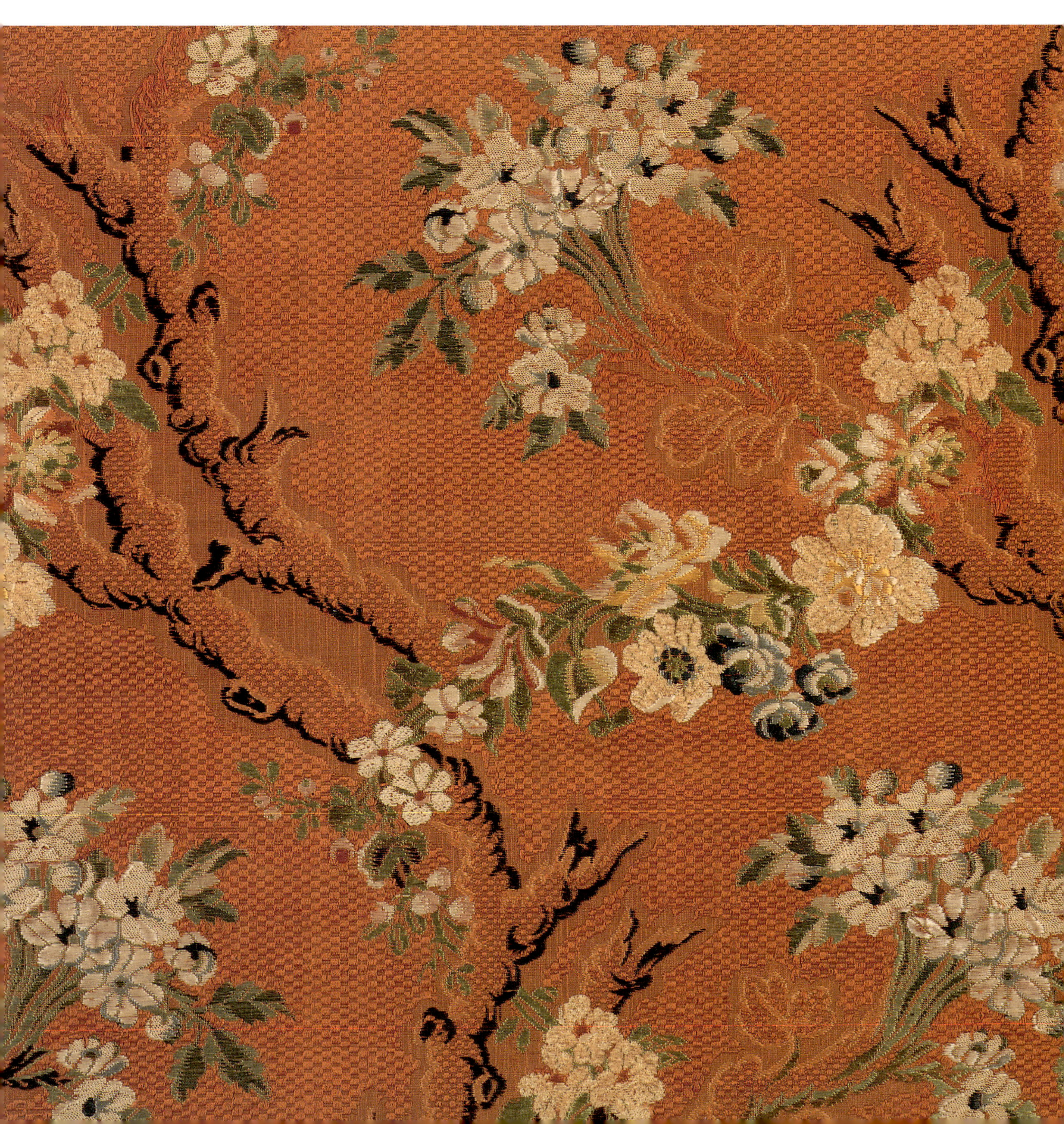

This was the situation that faced France in the seventeenth century. Fine textiles were produced there at that time, but the very best silks came from Italy. Sumptuary laws regulating expensive dress and requiring the use of domestically produced fabrics proved ineffectual. Finally, toward the end of the century, Louis xiv's chief minister, Jean-Baptiste Colbert, devised a plan to improve the French economy. An important part of his program was to make France the chief producer of luxury goods for all of Europe.

Silk-weaving companies were given subsidies and tax breaks. In addition, there were incentives to encourage highly skilled Italian silk weavers to immigrate to France. In some ways the situation was similar to that in America in the 1950s, when the best of Europe's scientific minds were persuaded to work in the United States. Although Italy passed laws forbidding emigration of skilled craftspersons and developed new styles of brocade fabric, France prevailed and in the eighteenth century was the undisputed leader of fashion for all of Europe.

To keep the lead, French silk producers had to maintain high standards of production, generate innovative designs, and make technological improvements to keep cost increases in labor and materials at a minimum. Owing to the popularity of large patterns and complex fabric structures, enriched in many cases by brocading, looms became very large and their operation required two or three men. Much attention was devoted to the automation of various aspects of textile production; indeed, this was the initial impetus for the Industrial Revolution. Many small advances were made during the eighteenth century, but the main problem—that pattern control required another person at the loom in addition to the weaver—was not solved until the beginning of the nineteenth century.

The silk manufacturers of Lyon hired Joseph-Marie Jacquard, the equivalent of today's textile engineer, to find a way to mechanize pattern control so it could be done by the weaver, thereby cutting labor costs. Jacquard invented for the loom a superstructure that controlled the pattern by means of perforated cards, allowing the weaver to regulate the pattern and weave at the same time. But although the French remained the unquestioned leaders in the production of luxury fabrics, it was the British who took the lead in textile automation and dominated mass production.

At the beginning of the nineteenth century, Kashmir shawls were becoming fashionable in Europe. These shawls, handwoven in India, had a fabric structure (twill tapestry) that is extremely labor-intensive. They were therefore very expensive and only the wealthy could afford them. Naturally, there was a potential market for a less expensive, but no less elegant, shawl. European weavers could make almost exact copies; however, their labor cost far more than that of the Indian weavers.

The solution was to re-create the tapestry-woven Kashmir shawl in a brocade structure. Undoubtedly the first brocaded "Kashmir" shawls were made in France on a drawloom, but soon these "imitation" shawls were being produced in other European weaving centers. The jacquard loom was ideal for such work, and as the card mechanism was perfected, shawls became even less expensive. Today we remember the European brocaded shawl by a town that became famous producing it—Paisley, Scotland.

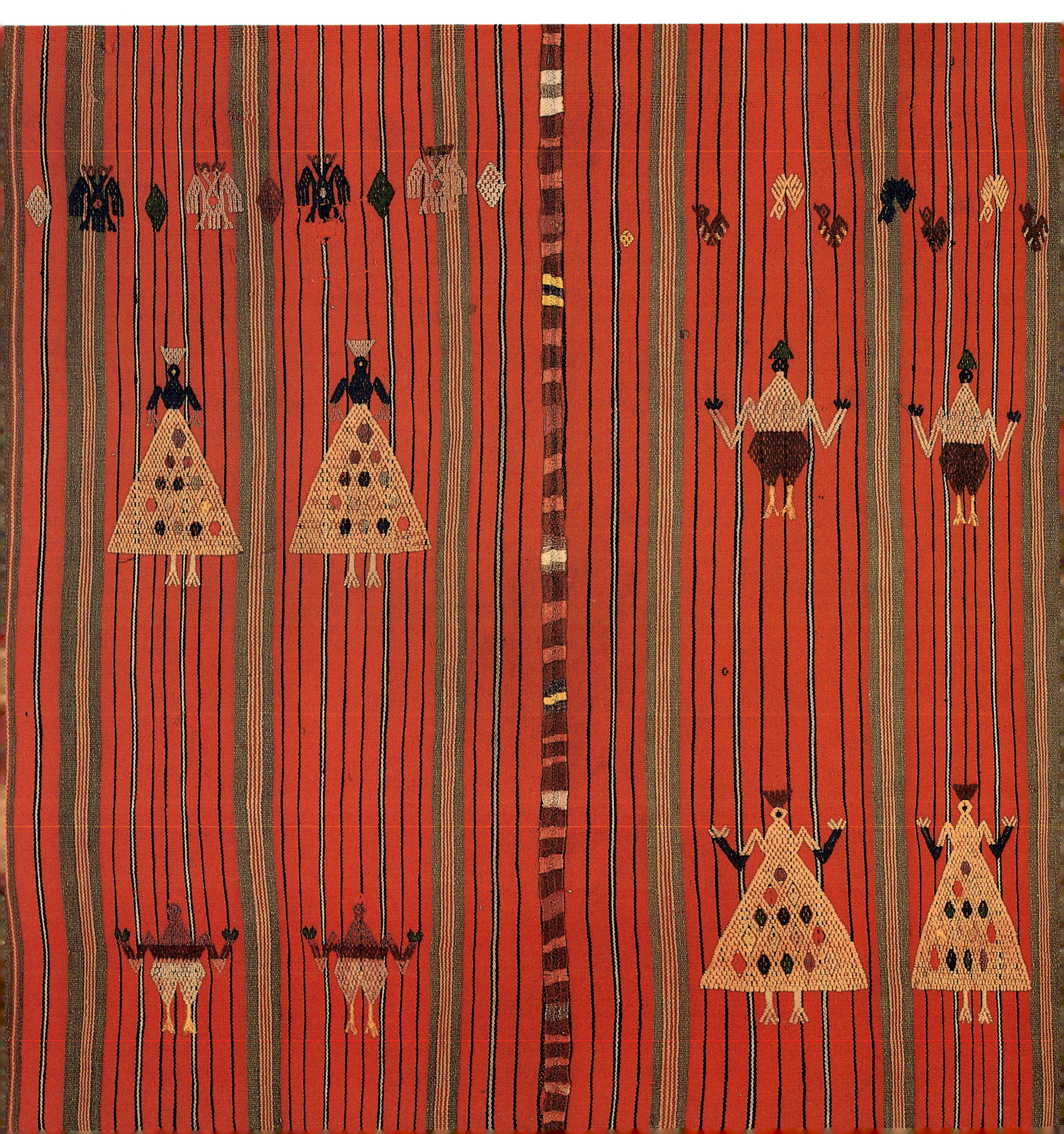

*Tzute* (carrying cloth), detail
Chichicastenango, Guatemala, 20th century
Cotton, silk, and wool
Gift of Elizabeth and Lloyd Olson   86.98.3

# The Americas

## Mesoamerica

Climatic conditions in Mesoamerica are unfavorable to cloth preservation, so it is difficult to determine just when brocaded textiles were first made in this area. Loom technology that would have permitted brocade weaving was fully developed in South America by 500 B.C. Knowledge of weaving spread northward, and textile remains found in La Candelaria cave indicate that weaving principles were well understood in northern Mexico by A.D. 1000.

In Mesoamerica before European contact, textiles were made primarily by women working in their homes on body-tension looms. Daughters learned to weave from their mothers. Beginning with narrow strips for belts and hair ribbons, they progressed to making blouse and skirt panels. With the Spanish occupation in the sixteenth century, the large, framed, horizontal loom was introduced. Small workshops outside the home were established and, as in Europe, men used this equipment. Both weaving traditions continue to this day; only rarely does a woman weave on the large horizontal loom or a man use the body-tension loom.

For the Indian population, clothing indicates regional affiliation and, to some degree, social status. Variations include width and length of blouses, skirts, shawls, hairbands, and belts for women and of shirts, pants, belts, and carrying cloths for men, as well as color combinations and decorative elements. Patterning is generally done on the loom by means of both inlay and weft float brocading techniques. In a few villages, notably Zacualpa in Guatemala, weft wrapping is also used.

Designs range from simple geometric diamond-shaped repeats to fanciful interpretations of birds and animals. Some villages have adapted European cross-stitch and embroidery patterns into their brocade weaving. Flower motifs have been especially popular. In certain areas, such as Chichicastenango in Guatemala, weavers sometimes form small, even loops with the brocade weft, which gives the appearance of uncut velvet.

Although many of the Indians' textile needs are met by cloth woven in the home, special textiles are sometimes purchased. Often these are produced in towns known for particular items. Totonicapán is a center that produces trade textiles for a number of different regions. The traditional patterns and colors of each region are used, so although the textiles are not woven locally they still identify the wearer as being from a specific locale.

In addition to the fabrics woven for individual regions, some Totonicapán weavers produce a distinctive type of brocade belt. This belt has a ground cloth of dark and light bands and is colorfully brocaded with "classic" traditional patterns interspersed with designs of the weaver's own invention—anything from cars and buses to helicopters and lettered inscriptions.

As inexpensive commercially produced textiles have become available, the practical need for domestically produced cloth has waned. Brocade weaving is still fairly common, but whether it will remain an important part of the culture is uncertain. Handwoven clothing still serves as a regional identifier, although in some areas the individual village styles are merging to form a style representative of a larger region. Weaving of especially fine pieces is encouraged by the willingness of collectors from the United States, Europe, and Japan to purchase superior textiles.

## The United States

Until the twentieth century, the weft float brocading technique used for the familiar blue-and-white or red-and-white overshot coverlets overshadowed all other handweaving in North America. Next to quilts, these coverlets were the most popular bedcoverings in the rural United States. The earliest examples that can be dated with certainty were made in the last quarter of the eighteenth century. They seem to have been inspired by coverlets brought by Scottish immigrants who came to America shortly after the Seven Years' War (1756–63). As the American textile industry developed, domestic production diminished,

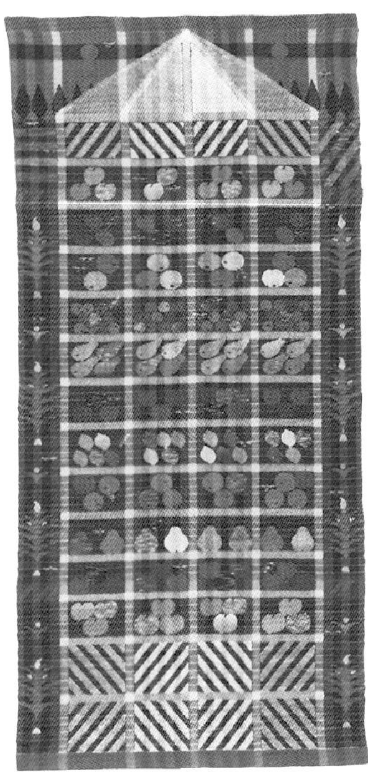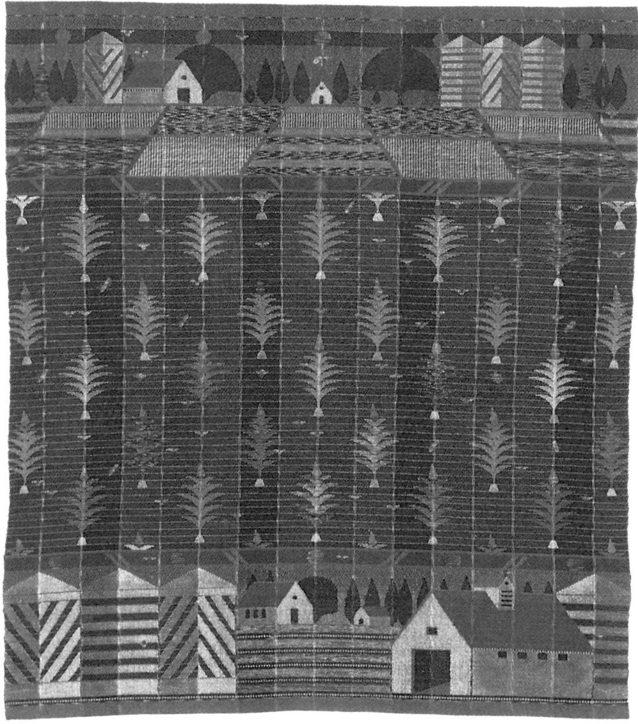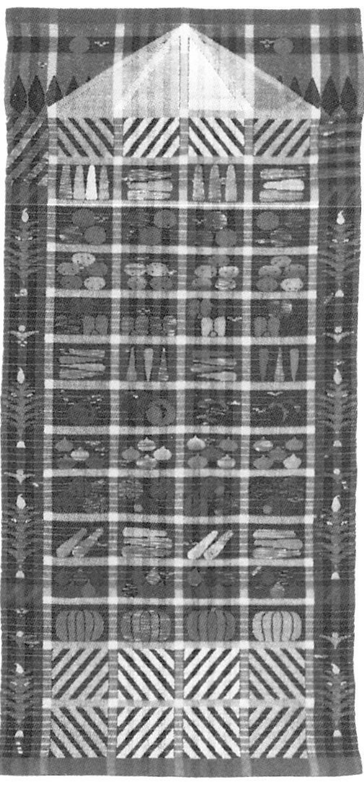

and few coverlets were made after the Civil War.

In addition to the relatively simple patterned coverlets produced by weavers working on shaft looms in their homes, more elaborately patterned coverlets were produced on jacquard looms by professional weavers in small towns. By the nineteenth century, most of the cotton thread generally used for construction of the ground cloth was commercially produced. The wool brocade weft that formed the design was often spun and dyed at home. This also was often the case for coverlets woven by professional weavers, because frequently the women placing the orders would provide the pattern thread.

During the last quarter of the nineteenth century, with commercially produced textiles available even in remote areas of the country, handweaving was no longer a practical necessity. During the 1930s, interest in weaving revived, but it was not until the late 1960s and concern over the effects of industrialization on the quality of our culture that handweaving began once again to have a life of its own. As appreciation of handwoven fabrics has grown, weavers have explored a variety of textile structures. In the mid to late 1980s, fiber artists have begun to use brocade structures. Creative exploration of brocade structures has been encouraged by the graduate program in fiber arts at Cranbrook Academy in Dearborn, Michigan. The Minneapolis Institute of Arts owns brocaded pieces by Gerhardt Knodel, director of the Fiber Arts Program, and by Morgan Clifford and Laura Foster Nicholson, two of the weavers who have completed this program.

In addition to the one-of-a-kind brocaded textiles handwoven in the 1980s, commercial brocade production has received new attention. Brocaded interior textiles, particularly upholstery fabrics, are now being manufactured. A number of museum collections throughout the country own fine examples produced by Jack Lenor Larsen, Inc.

For almost a century, brocaded textiles have had to take a back seat to printed fabrics. However, the last quarter of the twentieth century has seen a renewed interest in structural patterning, and it will be interesting to see how creatively industry, as well as textile artists, will make use of this very versatile weaving form.

Opposite: *Bounty and Thrift*, 1989
Laura Foster Nicholson, American (b. 1954)
Wool, silk, rayon, cotton, and synthetics
Gift of the Textile Council   89.59.1–3

Below: detail

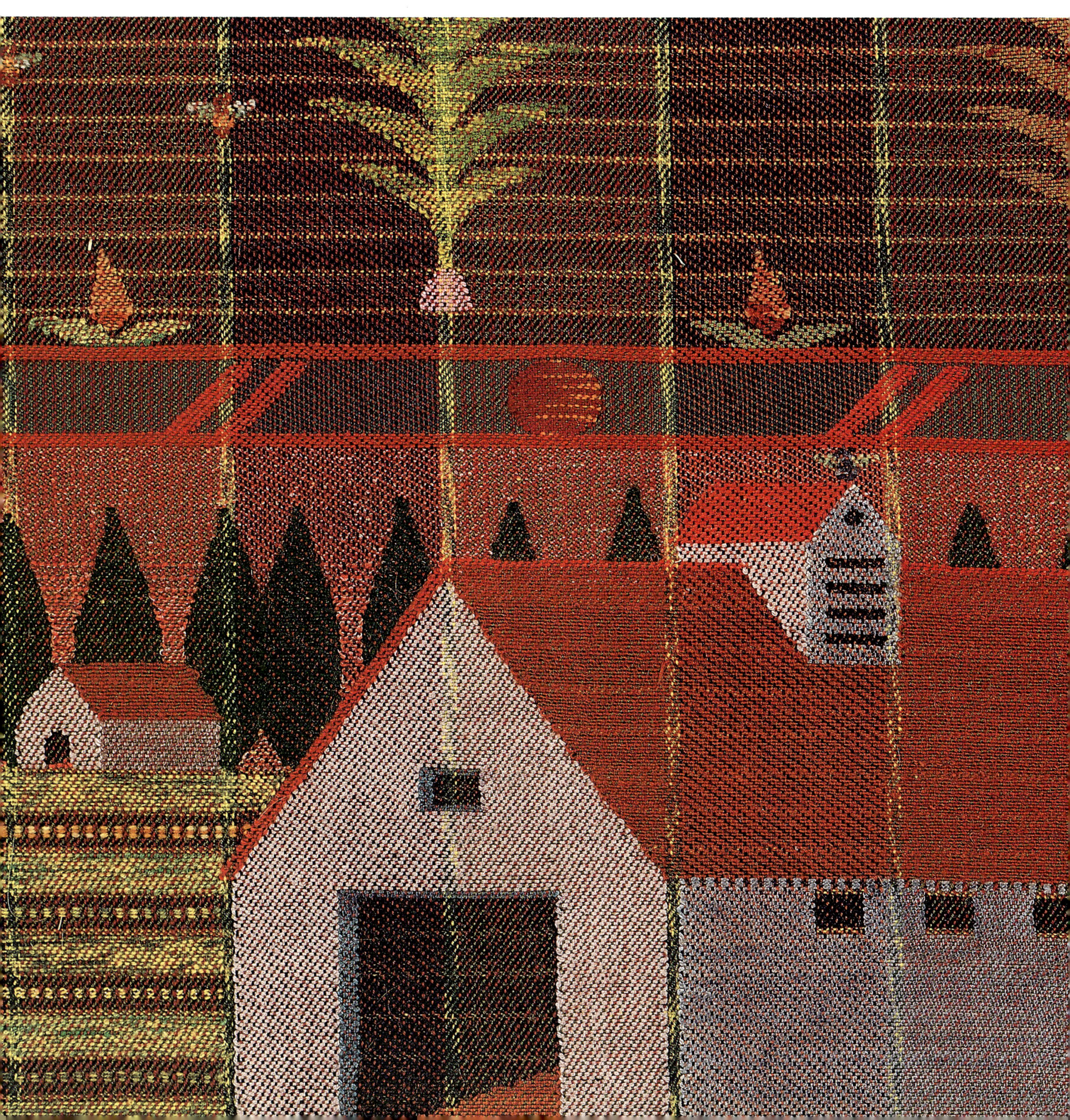

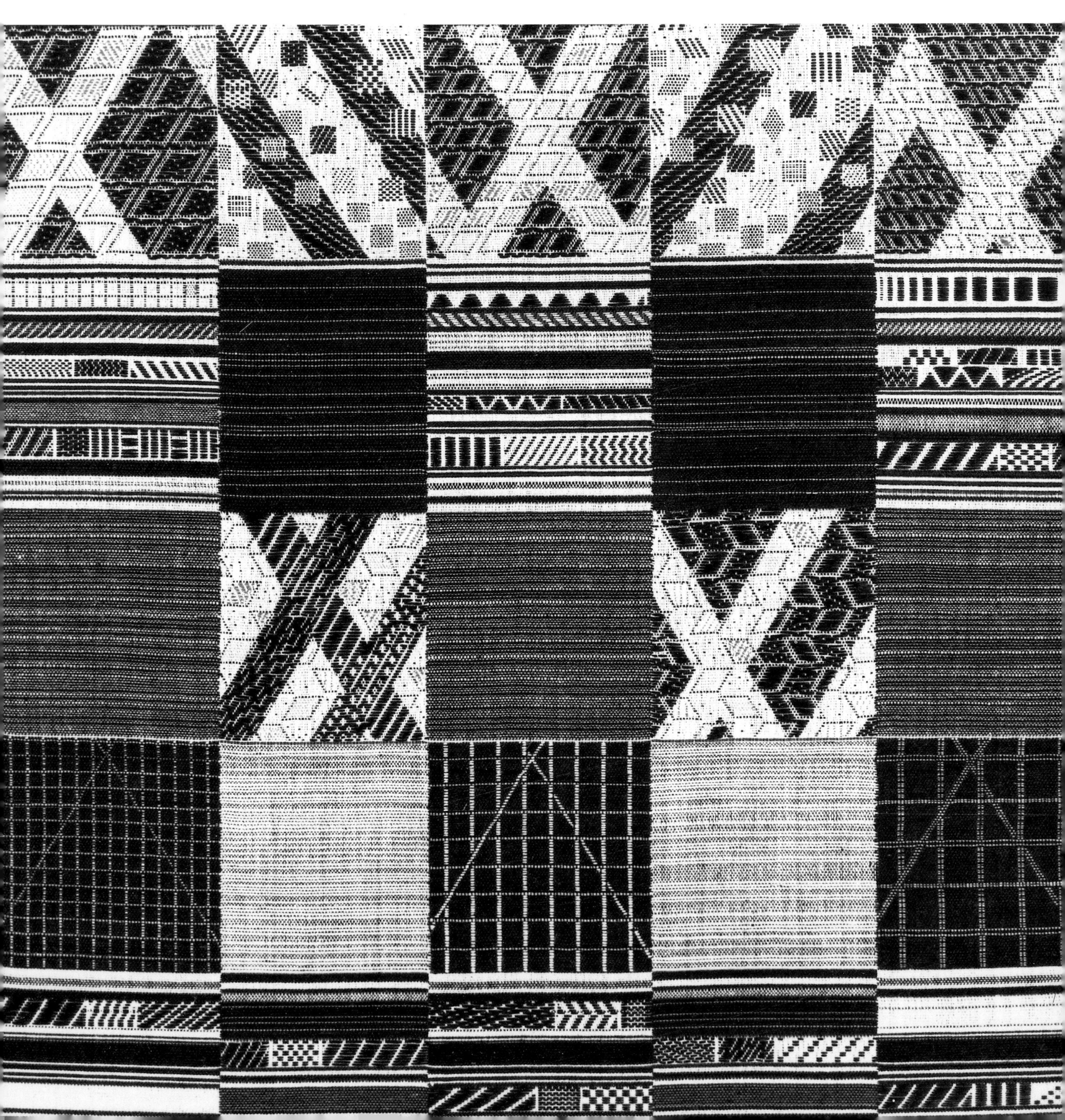


*Inside/Outside*, 1987, detail
Morgan Clifford, American (b. 1949)
Linen with metallic threads
Gift of Ellen and Fred Wells   88.39

# Brocading Techniques

Decorative cloth can be created in many ways. Printing and embroidery are embellishments added after the textile has been removed from the loom. With many woven structures, however, the decoration is incorporated during the weaving process. Brocade is a widely used structure for which this is the case. To understand the various techniques employed by the brocade weaver, one needs a basic knowledge of how cloth is made.

## The Woven Structure

A woven structure consists of two sets of threads, the warp and the weft, interlaced on a loom to form cloth. The warp stretches the length of the loom, under tension, and the weft is worked over and under it. Many different looms have been devised to meet specific needs, but all have two features in common: they enable the weaver to put tension on the warp threads, and they provide a mechanical means of separating the warp threads into two layers. The space formed between the upper and lower layers of the warp threads is called a shed.

To create a woven fabric, the weaver makes a shed using the loom's shedding mechanism and passes the weft through it from one edge of the warp to the other. Then the weaver makes a different shed, in which some of the warp threads that were previously on the upper layer become part of the lower layer. This locks the weft thread in place and also creates a new passage for it.

For the simplest cloth structure, only two different sheds are required. In the first shed every other warp thread is on the upper layer; in the second, or alternate, shed the threads of the upper layer change places with the threads of the lower layer. The cloth produced is called plain weave. It is easy to identify because the weft thread rests on top of every other warp thread of the fabric.

The structure of any woven fabric is determined by which warp threads are on top of the weft, forming the face of the cloth, and which are underneath the weft, on the reverse, or back, of the cloth. Some patterned fabrics have very complex woven structures, calling for many different sheds, and the looms for making them are equipped with complex shedding mechanisms. Other equally decorative cloth is quite simple and requires only a simple loom. Because brocade is a form of supplemental patterning, theoretically it can be either complex or simple. Its most popular use, however, has been in simple fabric structures.

The pattern of brocaded cloth is formed by supplementary threads that are added during the weaving process. These decorative threads are not essential to the primary, or basic, structure of the fabric. In this respect brocaded textiles are similar to embroidered cloth. In both, the decoration can be removed without altering the structural relationship of the warp and weft. Unlike the embroiderer, however, who can choose the order in which to execute the various elements of a design, the brocade weaver must build the pattern in horizontal sequence on the loom.

Brocade weaving is particularly challenging because all the decorative elements across any given horizontal line of the cloth must be considered almost simultaneously. If, for example, a cloth were to be decorated with a man and dog standing beside a tree, the embroiderer could easily work the image of the man first, then the tree trunk, then the tree's foliage, and finally the dog. An outer border might be added as a finishing touch. The brocade artist, in contrast, has to create the ground cloth and the decoration simultaneously. The weaver starts with warp threads under tension on the loom. First the essential weft of the ground cloth is passed through the correct shed. Then the brocade (nonessential) weft is passed through a different shed. The alternation of essential weft and brocade weft is carried on in all the areas where the pattern is to appear. To create the

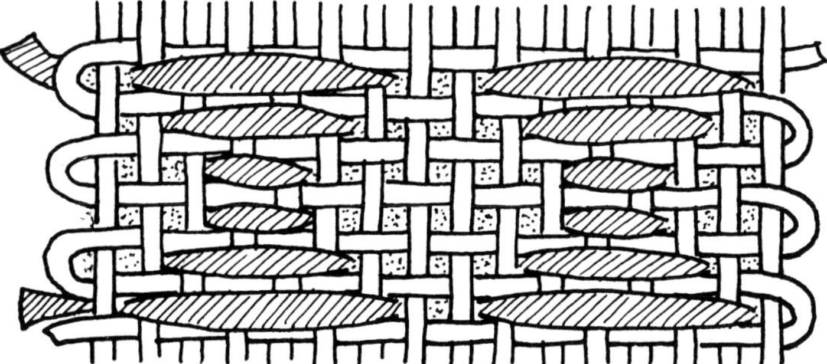

**Weft float brocade (face of fabric)**

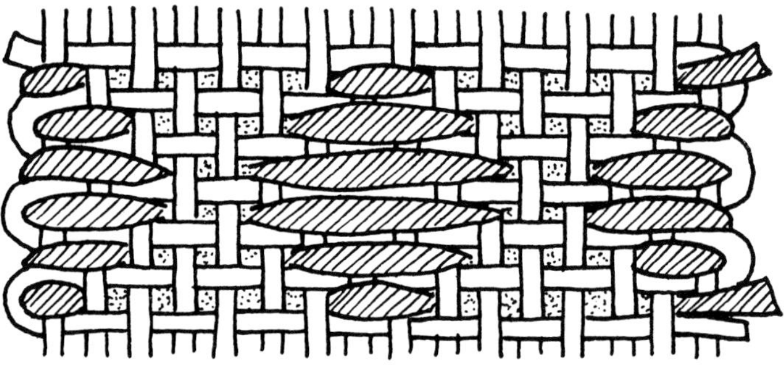

**Weft float brocade (reverse)**

image of man and dog beside a tree, the brocade weaver must begin the feet of the man, the base of the tree, and the paws of the dog, and also the border pattern, at the same time and continue developing the whole design in this manner through the weaving of the entire cloth.

In general, brocaded fabrics are designed so that the pattern is the dominant element and the ground cloth is the background. To emphasize this relationship, the brocade thread is frequently more loosely spun and of a slightly larger diameter than the warp and weft threads used in the ground cloth. As all the threads are placed in proper alignment, the brocade threads splay out to cover the essential threads (i.e., the warp and weft of the ground cloth).

The brocade weaver can incorporate the brocade weft in several different ways. The three most commonly used techniques are float brocading, inlay brocading, and weft wrapping.

## Float Brocading

Float brocading is probably the most widely used of the various brocading techniques. The Perugian towel from Italy and the *tampan* from Indonesia, pictured in this catalogue, are both examples of the float brocade structure. Some textile historians think that this technique may have developed as a way of reproducing the qualities of embroidery on the loom.

The pattern is formed by the brocade weft "floating" on top of the ground cloth. When not required for the design, the supplementary weft is pushed to the back side of the cloth, where it also floats, but is unseen when the face of the textile is viewed. Because the brocade thread is always visible on one or the other side of the cloth, some patterns have been developed that make the cloth reversible. An example is the overshot weave so popular with nineteenth-century American coverlet weavers. Reversible fabrics are sometimes referred to as double-faced brocades.

One of the inherent weaknesses of the float structure is the presence of long floats, which easily snag when the cloth is in use. In addition, long floats often sag, distorting lines that ought to be straight. To avoid these problems, patterns woven with the float technique are usually designed to minimize long brocade floats, often through the inclusion of small geometric elements. Such a use of adaptive design occurs in the rendering of the boat by the Sumatran weaver of the Indonesian *tampan*.

Sometimes, in addition to weft floats, supplementary warp threads are used to decorate a textile. They can be identified in the finished cloth as floats that lie parallel rather than perpendicular to the warp. Like weft floats, the supplementary warp threads are either on top of the ground cloth or floating at the back. The warp float is often seen in the elaborately patterned stripes of the silk fabrics used for men's coats (*kho*) in Bhutan.

## Inlay Brocading

Inlay brocade is used throughout the world but is particularly favored in areas where weaving technology is relatively simple, such as Guatemala and Bhutan. For all practical purposes the supplementary decorative threads are visible only on the face of the cloth, and thus these textiles are frequently referred to as single-sided brocades.

As with all brocades, the supplementary pattern thread is added after the primary weft has been placed. The weaver who uses the inlay technique will form the pattern shed from just one layer of the primary shed rather than selecting from all the warp threads. The pattern is often mechanically controlled through attachments to the loom but can also be woven with the use of a hand-held shed stick.

The advantage of the inlay brocade structure is that when supplementary threads do not appear on the face of the cloth as part of the pattern they are held securely between two layers of warp threads. This eliminates unsightly or structurally threatening floats on the reverse of the textile. In addition, single warp threads can easily be used to anchor long brocade wefts on the face of the cloth, making the fabric somewhat stronger and more durable while interfering but slightly with the overall pattern.

Inlay brocade has been used by the contemporary American weaver Laura Foster Nicholson, whose work is pictured in this catalogue.

## Weft Wrapping

Weft wrapping is especially prevalent in the Middle East, where its most popular form is called *soumak*. Because of its durability, weft wrapped brocade is used in the Middle East for floor, pillow, and door coverings and other household textiles and also for animal trappings. (A Caucasian horse covering is pictured in this catalogue.) The weft wrapped structure is also made by weavers in some regions of Guatemala, notably Zacualpa.

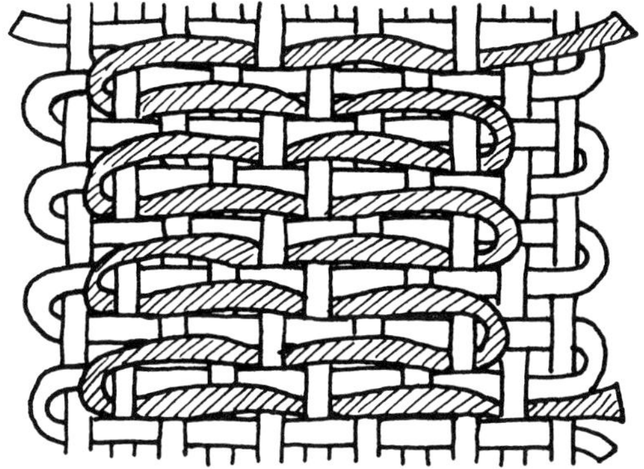

**Inlay brocade (face of fabric)**

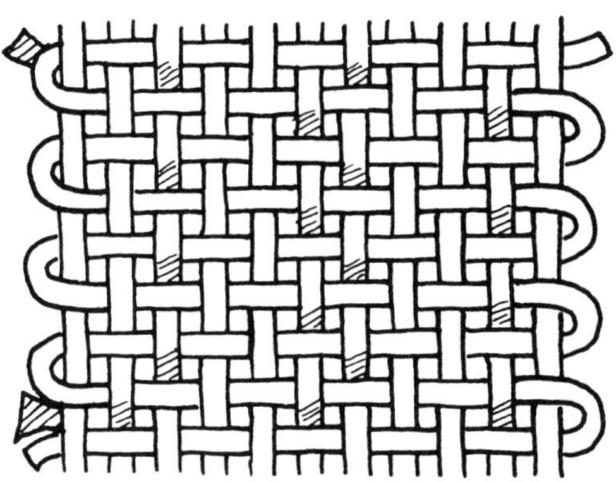

**Inlay brocade (reverse)**

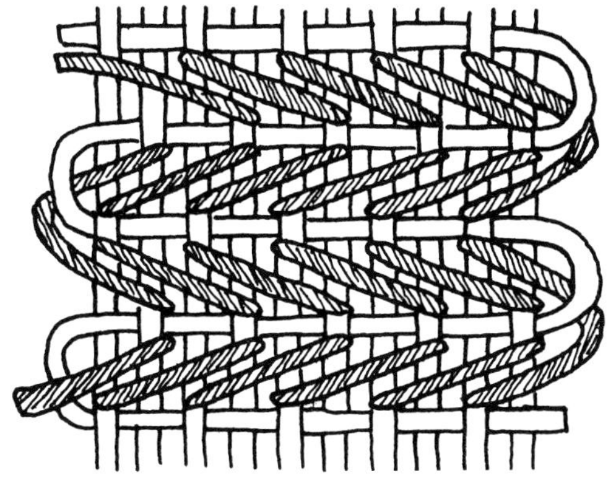

***Soumak*, a popular form of weft wrapping**

In weft wrapping, the brocade thread is wrapped around one or more warp threads. This changes the normal parallel relationship between the essential weft of the ground cloth and the brocade weft, so that a design made by weft wrapping has a diagonal or sometimes a herringbone look. And because weft wrapping requires more thread than other brocade structures, the pattern looks more three-dimensional than other brocades. Unlike other brocade structures, weft wrapping generally does not involve the use of secondary (brocade) sheds; instead, the weaver works from a single layer made up of all the warp threads. The necessity of manipulating the brocade thread by hand has prevented the mechanization of the weft wrapping technique.

Sometimes several structures are used in the same textile. European silk weavers often used a complex structure for the ground fabric and inlay brocade for selected decorative elements and would simply float the supplementary threads on the reverse of the cloth when they were not required for the pattern. With the exception of weft wrapping, it is often impossible to identify a particular brocade structure without seeing the reverse of the fabric.

## Discontinuous Supplementary Weft Brocading

In the brocade structures just discussed, the supplementary weft threads have been described as going from edge to edge of the ground cloth. A more time-consuming but frequently employed variation is the use of discontinuous supplementary weft threads: the brocade weft is introduced only in certain parts of the design and does not extend from one edge of the cloth to the other. This technique is particularly effective when the weaver wishes to use different colors along the same horizontal line. It can also be used to create lightweight and very delicate patterned fabrics. The Guatemalan weaver who wove the *tzute* on page 22, and Laura Foster Nicholson, whose wall hanging is illustrated on pages 24 and 25, both used discontinuous supplemenary weft threads to create elaborate patterns.

Most brocade designs consist of horizontally repeating elements because such patterns can be efficiently executed with brocading techniques. This is especially true when the pattern sheds are mechanically controlled rather than hand selected. Patterns woven on looms with mechanically controlled shedding devices often call for several pattern sheds for every one essential weft when several colors are used along one horizontal line. For instance, European weavers created shaded leaves by using light green thread for one half of the leaf and dark green for the other half. To accomplish this, they had to weave one essential weft of the ground fabric, one light green discontinuous brocade thread and one dark green discontinuous brocade thread, and then add the next essential weft. These steps were repeated until the design no longer called for two colors.

When the cost of labor is high, textiles decorated by means of discontinuous brocading are often more expensive than those woven with simpler brocading techniques, because they usually take quite a lot longer to weave. On the other hand, when materials are more costly than labor, discontinuous weft patterning can reduce the expense of metallic and other luxury threads, since such threads are used only where the design requires them and do not float unseen on the back of the fabric.

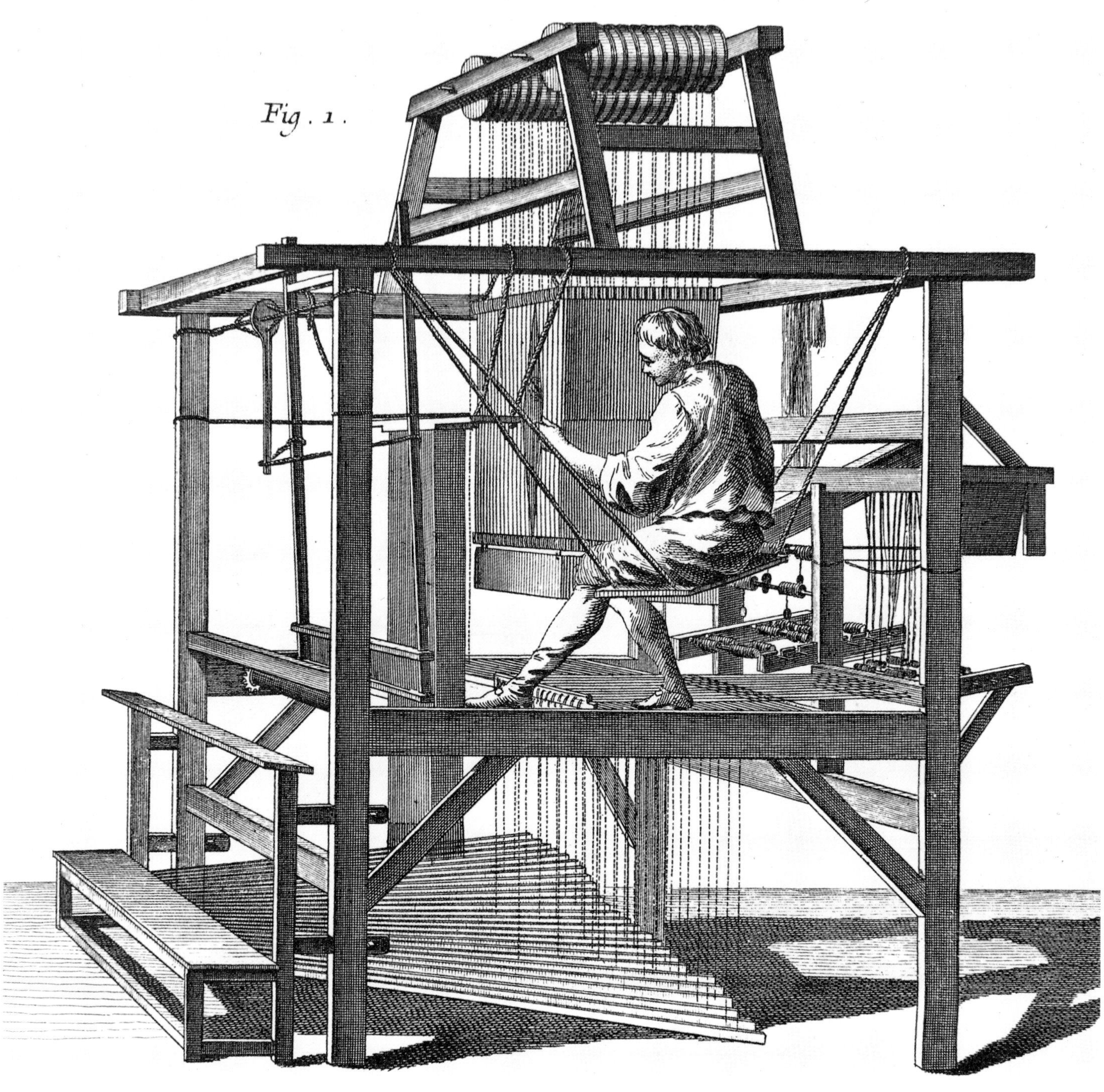

A loom used in eighteenth-century Europe to weave elaborate ribbons and trims (*passementeries*), many of which were brocaded. (Diderot, *Encyclopédie*)

# Appendix: Brocaded Textiles in The Minneapolis Institute of Arts

The first textiles with supplementary woven patterning acquired by The Minneapolis Institute of Arts were a few European brocades, which were purchased even before a museum had been built to house the Institute's collections. This modest beginning was augmented in 1920 with a gift from Mrs. Charles C. Bovey of 60 seventeenth- and eighteenth-century brocaded silks, most of them woven in Italy or France. A new dimension was added when Miss Lily Place gave some Middle Eastern examples that she had acquired in the 1920s, while living in Egypt. Another active collector during that period, Mrs. Stanley Hawks, the wife of a diplomat who served in Guatemala in the late 1920s, acquired a number of pieces with the assistance of Lilly de Jongh Osborne. Her collection came to the museum in 1978. The 1980s have been active years, with purchases of European silks and gifts from several private individuals. Roberta and Richard Simmons have been particularly generous with donations of Guatemalan pieces and have provided all our holdings of West African textiles, some of which are brocaded.

In the review which follows, notes on the continuing development of the textile collection indicate general additions to the holdings in a particular area, not an effort to acquire brocaded textiles as such.

## The Middle East

All but one of the museum's fifteen Middle Eastern brocades are domestic textiles created by nomadic weavers around the turn of the century. Five of the fifteen pieces were made in the Caucasus, four in Persia, and six in Turkey. A number of local rug collectors own some fine *soumak* and *cicim* pieces, but at present the museum is not actively collecting in this area.

## Asia

Of the seventy-six Asian woven pieces patterned predominately with brocading, thirteen were woven in China, three in Japan, four in Indonesia, fifteen in India, forty in Bhutan, and one in Sri Lanka. Although a few are eighteenth-century, most represent traditions of the nineteenth century, with the exception of the Bhutanese material, which is most likely all twentieth-century. (Satisfactory dating criteria have not yet been established for Bhutanese textiles.) The museum occasionally adds Asian textiles to its collection as opportunities arise, but is not actively seeking them at this time. There are a number of fine pieces, especially from Indonesia, in local private collections.

## West Africa

The museum owns nine West African brocaded pieces, from Ghana, Niger, Nigeria, and Mali, all made in the twentieth century. A local private collector is actively acquiring African textiles, and the Institute's holdings in this area will most likely continue to grow.

## Europe

Of the approximately one hundred pieces of European brocade, most are silks made in France and Italy during the seventeenth and eighteenth centuries. There are also a few Dutch, Spanish, and English examples. Many of these fabrics have a complex structure, with two or more warps and wefts making up the ground cloth. The pieces range in size from small fragments 5 by 9 inches to large panels 23 by 115 inches. There are also four cotton and linen towels from the Umbrian region of Italy. The museum continues to collect European textiles.

## The Americas

Brocades from the Americas fall into three groups. The largest comprises eighty-five Guatemalan pieces, most of them untailored costumes woven by women on body-tension looms. There are a few pre-Columbian fragments, valuable as study pieces exemplifying the brocade technique. And ten pieces were woven in the United States: six and a half overshot brocaded coverlets (two and a half made on shaft looms, four on jacquard looms) and four pieces by contemporary fiber artists (Morgan Clifford, Gerhardt Knodel, Jack Lenor Larsen, and Laura Foster Nicholson). There are several private collectors of Guatemalan textiles in our area. The museum will probably continue to expand its Guatemalan holdings and also its holdings of contemporary weavings by U.S. artists, purchases of which are supported in part by the Textile Council.

# Suggested Reading

### The Middle East

Cootner, Cathryn. *Flat-woven Textiles*. The Arthur D. Jenkins Collection, vol. 1. Washington, D.C.: Textile Museum, 1981.

### South Asia

Cort, Cynthia R. Cunningham. "The Brocades of Banaras." *Bulletin of the Needle and Bobbin Club* 63, nos. 1, 2 (1980): 3–35.

Myers, Diana K. "Costume and Ceremonial Textiles of Bhutan." *Textile Museum Journal 1987* 26 (1988): 25–53.

### The Far East

Minnich, Helen Benton, in collaboration with Shojiro Nomura. *Japanese Costume and the Makers of Its Elegant Tradition*. Rutland, Vt., and Tokyo, Japan: Charles E. Tuttle Co., 1963.

Wilson, Verity. *Chinese Dress*. London: Victoria and Albert Museum, 1986.

### West Africa

Lamb, Venice. *West African Weaving*. London: Duckworth, 1975.

Picton, John, and John Mack. *African Textiles: Looms, Weaving, and Design*. London: British Museum Publications, 1979.

### Europe

Carlano, Marianne, and Larry Salmon, eds. *French Textiles: From the Middle Ages through the Second Empire*. Hartford, Conn.: Wadsworth Atheneum, 1985.

Fanelli, Rosalia Bonito. *Five Centuries of Italian Textiles: 1300–1800*. Prato, Italy: Museo del Tessuto, 1981.

### The Americas

Burnham, Harold B., and Dorothy K. Burnham. *"Keep Me Warm One Night": Early Handweaving in Eastern Canada*. Toronto and Buffalo: University of Toronto Press in cooperation with the Royal Ontario Museum, 1972.

O'Neale, Lila M. *Textiles of Highland Guatemala*. Publication 567, Carnegie Institution of Washington, Washington, D.C., 1945. Reprint. New York: Johnson Reprint Corporation, 1976.

### Brocading Techniques

Baizerman, Suzanne, and Karen Searle. *Latin American Brocades: Explorations in Supplementary Weft Techniques*. St. Paul, Minn.: Dos Tejedoras, 1976.

Tidball, Harriet. *Brocade*. Shuttle Craft Guild Monograph 22. Santa Ana, Calif.: HTH Publishers, 1968. (Currently published by Shuttle Craft Books, Coupeville, Wash.)

# Exhibition Staff

Evan Maurer, *Director*
Timothy Fiske, *Associate Director*
Michael Conforti, *Chief Curator; Bell Memorial
	Curator of Decorative Arts and Sculpture*
Lotus Stack, *Curator of Textiles; curator in charge
	of exhibition*
Mary Ann Butterfield, *Associate Conservator,
	Textiles*
Peggy Dorwick and Beverly Hussian,
	*Administrative Assistants, Textiles*
Robert Jacobsen, *Curator, Asian Art*
Catherine Parker, *Curatorial Assistant, Asian Art*
Beth Desnick, *Exhibitions Coordinator*
Kathryn C. Johnson, *Chair, Education Division*
Lisa Nebenzahl, *Media Producer*
James Ockuly, *Media Production Assistant*
Gary Mortensen, *Photographer*
Robert Fogt, *Photographic Technician*
Elisabeth Sövik, *Associate Editor*
Anne Knauff, *Assistant Designer*
Patrick Atherton, *Typesetter*
Nancy Perron, *Director of Public Relations*
Muriel Morrisette, *Associate Director, Public
	Relations*
Alla Litkewitsch, *Administrative Assistant,
	Public Relations*
Kathy Hedberg, *Public Relations Assistant*
Laura DeBiaso, *Scheduling Coordinator*
Gwen Bitz, *Registrar*
Karen Duncan, *Associate Registrar*
Claire Ouellette, *Assistant Registrar for the
	Permanent Collection*
Shawn Spurgin, *Registration Assistant*
Roxy Ballard, *Exhibition Designer*
Steven Williams, *Lighting Technician*
Susan Wood, *Collection Maintenance Technician*
Ken Krenz, *Storage Technician*
Tom Jance, *Chief Exhibition Technician*
Charles Foster, Patti Landres, William Skodje,
	Brian Stieler, *Exhibition Technicians*
Jan Blanchard, *Maintenance Supervisor*
Gordon Cable, *Chief of Security*